I0504675

Starting a Food Truck Business

LIAM LUXE

Copyright © 2023 Liam Luxe

All rights reserved.

CONTENTS

INTRODUCTION

Food trucks have become a ubiquitous sight on the streets of many cities, offering a wide variety of cuisines and flavors to hungry customers. The food truck industry has grown rapidly in recent years, fueled by a desire for unique and high-quality food experiences, the appeal of mobile dining, and the entrepreneurial spirit of food lovers. If you're reading this book, you're likely considering starting a food truck business of your own, and we're here to help. In this guide, we'll provide you with the knowledge and tools you need to start your own successful food truck business, from market research and planning to menu development and financial management. Whether you're a seasoned chef or a food enthusiast looking to turn your passion into a business, this book will give you the insights and guidance you need to get started. So let's get cooking!

What is a food truck business?

A food truck business is a mobile eatery that serves food to customers on the go. Unlike traditional restaurants, food trucks are typically small, mobile vehicles that are equipped with cooking equipment and supplies to prepare and serve food. Food trucks are known for offering a wide variety of food, ranging from classic street food such as tacos and hot dogs, to more gourmet options like artisanal sandwiches and fusion dishes.

Food truck businesses are becoming increasingly popular, as they offer several benefits compared to traditional brick-and-mortar restaurants. For example, food trucks have lower overhead costs since they don't require a permanent physical location, and they can move to different locations throughout the day to reach more customers. This flexibility also allows food truck operators to take advantage of popular events or locations, such as festivals, concerts, and busy street corners.

Starting a food truck business can be a great option for aspiring entrepreneurs who are passionate about food and want to share their culinary creations with a wider audience. It's a challenging but rewarding endeavor that requires careful planning, hard work, and a willingness to adapt to changing circumstances. In the following chapters, we'll provide you with the information and guidance you need to get started on your food truck journey.

Advantages and disadvantages of starting a food truck business

Starting a food truck business has both advantages and disadvantages. Here are some of the main ones to consider:

Advantages:

- **Lower overhead costs:** Compared to brick-and-mortar restaurants, food trucks have lower overhead costs, which can make them a more affordable option for aspiring entrepreneurs. You don't have to pay for a physical storefront, and you can save money on utilities, rent, and other expenses.

- **Flexibility:** Food trucks offer a level of flexibility that is hard to match with traditional restaurants. You can move your business to different locations throughout the day to reach more customers, and you can also take advantage of popular events or locations, such as festivals, concerts, and busy street corners.

- **Unique food experiences:** Food trucks are known for offering a wide variety of food, ranging from classic street food to more gourmet options. By starting a food truck business, you can share your culinary creations with a wider audience and offer unique and high-quality food experiences.

- **Marketing opportunities:** A food truck can be a great marketing tool for your brand. By driving around town and participating in events, you can increase brand awareness and reach a larger audience.

Disadvantages:

- **Limited space:** Food trucks have limited space for cooking and storing food, which can make it challenging to prepare complex or large-scale dishes. You'll need to carefully plan your menu and make sure that you have all the equipment and supplies you need to prepare and serve your food.

- **Weather conditions:** Weather conditions can have a significant impact on your business. If it's too hot, too cold, or too rainy, customers may not want to wait outside for food. You'll need to plan accordingly and have a backup plan in case of inclement weather.

- **Permits and regulations:** Starting a food truck business requires obtaining permits and complying with regulations set by local and state authorities. These requirements can vary depending on your location, and they can be time-consuming and expensive to navigate.

- **Maintenance and repair costs:** Food trucks require regular maintenance and repairs to keep them in good working condition. This can add up to significant costs over time, and you'll need to factor these expenses into your budget.

Starting a food truck business has both advantages and disadvantages. It's important to carefully consider these factors and weigh the pros and cons before deciding if a food truck is the right option for you.

MARKET RESEARCH AND PLANNING

Market research and planning are crucial steps when starting a food truck business. By conducting market research, you can identify your target customers, understand their preferences and needs, and develop a menu and marketing strategy that will appeal to them. Planning, on the other hand, involves creating a roadmap for your business, setting goals, and developing a budget and timeline for launching and growing your food truck business. In this section, we'll explore the importance of market research and planning and provide you with practical tips and strategies to help you get started.

Identifying your target market

One of the most important steps in starting a food truck business is identifying your target market. Your target market is the group of customers that you want to reach and serve with your food truck. By understanding your target market, you can develop a menu and marketing strategy that will appeal to their preferences and needs.

Here are some tips for identifying your target market:

Analyze demographics: Start by analyzing the demographics of the area where you plan to operate your food truck. Look at factors such as age, gender, income, and education level. This information can help you identify the types of customers who are most likely to be interested in your food.

Consider location: The location of your food truck can also have a significant impact on your target market. If you plan to operate near a college or university, for example, your target market may be college students who are looking for affordable and convenient meal options.

Analyze competitors: Look at the food trucks and restaurants that are already operating in your area. What types of food do they offer? Who are their customers? By analyzing your competitors, you can identify gaps in the market and opportunities to differentiate your food truck.

Conduct surveys: Consider conducting surveys or focus groups to gather feedback from potential customers. Ask questions about their food preferences, dining habits, and willingness to try new foods. This information can help you refine your menu and marketing strategy.

Consider food trends: Finally, consider current food trends and popular cuisine styles when developing your menu. Are there any up-and-coming food trends that you can capitalize on? Is there a particular cuisine style that is popular in your area?

Identifying your target market is a crucial step in starting a successful food truck business. By analyzing demographics, location, competitors, and food trends, you can develop a menu and marketing strategy that will appeal to your target customers and set your business up for success.

Conducting market research

Conducting market research is a crucial step in starting a food truck business. It involves gathering and analyzing information about your target market, competitors, and industry trends. By conducting market research, you can identify opportunities and challenges, develop a menu and marketing strategy that will appeal to your customers, and make informed decisions about your business.

Here are some steps for conducting market research:

Define your research objectives: Start by defining your research objectives. What do you want to learn from your market research? Are you trying to understand customer preferences, identify gaps in the market, or analyze competitors? Defining your research objectives will help you focus your research and gather the information you need.

Gather data: There are several methods you can use to gather data for your market research. You can conduct surveys, focus groups, and interviews with potential customers, analyze data from online sources, or gather data from industry reports and publications. Consider using a combination of methods to gather a broad range of data.

Analyze the data: Once you've gathered data, you need to analyze it to draw conclusions and make informed decisions. Look for patterns and trends in the data, identify gaps in the market, and consider how you can use the data to develop a menu and marketing strategy that will appeal to your customers.

Refine your business plan: Based on your market research, refine your business plan to reflect your findings. Consider adjusting your menu, pricing, and marketing strategy to better align with the needs and preferences of your target market. You may also need to adjust your budget and timeline based on your findings.

Creating a business plan

Creating a business plan is an essential step in starting a food truck business. A business plan is a written document that outlines your business goals, strategies, and operations. It serves as a roadmap for your business, helping you stay on track and make informed decisions. Here are some key components to include in your food truck business plan:

Executive summary: This is a brief overview of your business plan, including your business goals, target market, and financial projections.

Company description: Describe your food truck business and its unique features. What sets your food truck apart from others in the market?

Market analysis: Conduct a thorough market analysis and identify your target market. Analyze the competition and their strengths and weaknesses. Identify gaps in the market that you can fill.

Menu and pricing strategy: Develop a menu that aligns with your target market's preferences and dietary restrictions. Develop a pricing strategy that is competitive and profitable.

Marketing and sales strategy: Develop a marketing and sales strategy that will help you reach your target market. This may include social media marketing, events, and promotions.

Operations plan: Develop an operations plan that outlines how you will run your food truck business. This includes your staffing plan, inventory management, and equipment needs.

Financial projections: Develop financial projections for your food truck business, including startup costs, ongoing expenses, and revenue projections.

Creating a business plan can be time-consuming, but it's a critical step in starting a successful food truck business. It will help you stay focused, make informed decisions, and secure funding if necessary.

Deciding on your food truck concept

Deciding on your food truck concept is a critical step in starting a food truck business. Your concept will set you apart from other food trucks in the market and help you attract your target market. Here are some factors to consider when deciding on your food truck concept:

Identify your niche: Identify a unique niche that you can fill in the market. This may involve offering a particular cuisine, such as Mexican, Thai, or vegan food, or catering to a particular audience, such as college students or health-conscious individuals.

Consider your target market: Consider your target market when developing your food truck concept. What are their preferences and dietary restrictions? What type of food is popular in the area where you will be operating?

Keep it simple: Keep your menu simple and focused. This will help you manage your inventory and reduce waste. Consider offering a few signature dishes and rotating specials.

Use high-quality ingredients: Use high-quality ingredients to create delicious and memorable dishes. Consider sourcing ingredients locally to support the community and promote sustainability.

Consider branding and marketing: Develop a brand that reflects your food truck concept and target market. Use social media and other marketing channels to promote your business and attract customers.

Overall, deciding on your food truck concept is a critical step in starting a successful food truck business. By identifying your niche, considering your target market, keeping your menu simple, using high-quality ingredients, and developing a strong brand and marketing strategy, you can set yourself apart from the competition and attract loyal customers.

LEGAL REQUIREMENTS AND PERMITS

Starting a food truck business involves complying with a variety of legal requirements and obtaining the necessary permits. This can be a complex process, but it's essential to ensure that your business is operating legally and safely. In this section, we'll explore the key legal requirements and permits that you need to start a food truck business, and provide tips on how to navigate the process.

Registering your business

Before you start operating your food truck, you need to register your business with the appropriate government agencies. Registering your business ensures that it is recognized as a legal entity and allows you to comply with tax laws and other regulations. Here are some steps to follow when registering your food truck business:

Choose a business name: Choose a unique and memorable name for your food truck business. Make sure that the name is not already taken by checking with the appropriate government agency.

Register your business: Register your business with the appropriate government agency. This may be the state or local government, depending on where you will be operating your food truck. You may need to register your business as a sole proprietorship, LLC, or corporation.

Obtain a tax ID number: Obtain a tax ID number, also known as an employer identification number (EIN), from the IRS. This number is required for tax purposes and allows you to open a business bank account.

Apply for permits and licenses: Apply for the necessary permits and licenses to operate your food truck legally. This may include a food service establishment permit, health department permit, and business license. Requirements vary depending on your location, so check with your local government agency for specific requirements.

Registering your food truck business can be a time-consuming process, but it's essential for ensuring that your business is operating legally and can protect you from legal issues in the future. By following these steps, you can register your business and obtain the necessary permits and licenses to start operating your food truck.

Obtaining licenses and permits

Obtaining the necessary licenses and permits is a critical step in starting a food truck business. These licenses and permits ensure that your food truck is operating safely and legally and can help you avoid costly fines and legal issues. Here are some of the licenses and permits that you may need to obtain to operate your food truck:

Food service establishment permit: This permit is required for any business that prepares and serves food to the public. The permit is issued by the local health department and ensures that your food truck meets the necessary health and safety requirements.

Health department permit: In addition to the food service establishment permit, you may also need to obtain a health department permit. This permit is issued by the local health department and ensures that your food truck meets the necessary health and safety regulations.

Business license: You may need to obtain a business license to operate your food truck. This license is issued by the local government and ensures that your business is recognized as a legal entity.

Parking permit: You may need to obtain a parking permit to operate your food truck in a specific location. This permit is issued by the local government and ensures that you are allowed to park and operate your food truck in a particular area.

Fire and safety permits: You may need to obtain fire and safety permits to ensure that your food truck meets the necessary fire and safety regulations.

The requirements for licenses and permits vary depending on your location, so it's essential to check with your local government agency to determine the specific requirements for your food truck. Obtaining the necessary licenses and permits can be a time-consuming process, but it's crucial for ensuring that your food truck is operating legally and safely.

Meeting health and safety regulations

By ensuring that your food truck meets the necessary health and safety regulations, you can protect your customers and your business from potential health hazards and legal issues. Here are some tips for meeting health and safety regulations:

Follow food safety guidelines: Make sure that you are following the appropriate food safety guidelines when preparing and serving food. This includes properly storing, cooking, and handling food to prevent contamination and foodborne illnesses.

Keep your food truck clean: Regularly clean and sanitize your food truck to prevent the buildup of dirt, grease, and bacteria. This includes cleaning food preparation surfaces, equipment, and utensils.

Train your staff: Ensure that your staff is properly trained in food safety and hygiene practices. This can include training on proper handwashing techniques, cooking temperatures, and safe food handling procedures.

Maintain proper temperature control: Proper temperature control is essential for preventing foodborne illnesses. Make sure that your food is stored and served at the appropriate temperatures to prevent the growth of bacteria.

Display food safety certifications: Display any food safety certifications or permits that you have obtained in a visible location in your food truck. This can help to build trust with your customers and show that you are committed to meeting health and safety regulations.

Meeting health and safety regulations is crucial for ensuring the success of your food truck business. By following these tips, you can ensure that your food truck is operating safely and can avoid potential health hazards and legal issues.

FINANCING YOUR FOOD TRUCK BUSINESS

Starting a food truck business requires a significant amount of upfront capital to cover expenses such as purchasing a food truck, equipment, permits, licenses, and inventory. Financing your food truck business can be a challenging task, but with the right approach and strategy, you can secure the funds you need to get your business off the ground. In this section, we will explore various financing options available for starting a food truck business and provide tips on how to secure the funding you need.

Estimating startup costs

Estimating the startup costs is a crucial step in starting a food truck business. It will give you an idea of how much capital you will need to get your business up and running. Here are some of the expenses you will need to consider when estimating your startup costs:

Purchasing a food truck: The cost of purchasing a food truck can vary depending on the size, condition, and customization of the vehicle. On average, a new food truck can cost between $50,000 and $200,000.

Equipment: You will need to purchase equipment such as a refrigerator, stove, griddle, and fryer. The cost of equipment can vary depending on the quality and brand.

Permits and licenses: You will need to obtain permits and licenses to operate your food truck legally. The cost of permits and licenses can vary depending on your location.

Inventory: You will need to purchase ingredients and supplies to prepare and serve your menu items.

Marketing and branding: You will need to invest in marketing and branding to promote your food truck and build brand awareness.

When estimating your startup costs, it's important to be as accurate as possible. This will help you avoid underestimating your expenses and running out of capital before your business has a chance to become profitable. By estimating your startup costs, you can determine how much capital you need to secure and which financing options may be the best fit for your business.

Funding options

There are various funding options available for financing your food truck business. Here are some of the most common options:

Self-funding: Self-funding involves using your own savings or personal assets to finance your business. This option allows you to maintain control over your business and avoid debt. However, it may not be feasible for everyone, and it can be risky to invest all of your personal funds into a business.

Small Business Administration (SBA) loans: The SBA offers loans to small businesses with lower interest rates and longer repayment terms than traditional loans. These loans can be used to finance various expenses, including equipment purchases and working capital.

Crowdfunding: Crowdfunding involves raising funds from a large number of people through online platforms such as Kickstarter and Indiegogo. Crowdfunding can help you raise capital quickly, but it requires a lot of effort and marketing to be successful.

Angel investors: Angel investors are individuals or groups who invest in early-stage businesses in exchange for equity or ownership. Angel investors can provide significant capital and expertise to help grow your business.

Traditional loans: Traditional loans from banks or credit unions can be used to finance your food truck business. These loans often require collateral and have higher interest rates than SBA loans.

When choosing a funding option for your food truck business, it's important to consider the amount of capital you need, your credit score, and your business plan. Each funding option has its advantages and disadvantages, and it's important to choose the option that best fits your needs and goals.

Creating a budget

Creating a budget is an essential step in starting and running a successful food truck business. A budget is a financial plan that outlines your expected income and expenses. Here are some steps to help you create a budget for your food truck business:

List your expenses: List all the expenses you expect to incur, including equipment, food and supplies, permits and licenses, insurance, marketing, and any other expenses.

Estimate your income: Estimate your income based on your menu pricing, sales projections, and any other revenue sources such as catering events or festivals.

Identify fixed and variable costs: Identify which expenses are fixed, meaning they stay the same each month, and which expenses are variable, meaning they fluctuate depending on sales volume.

Determine your break-even point: Your break-even point is the amount of revenue you need to cover all your expenses. This can help you set realistic sales goals and make informed decisions about pricing and promotions.

Adjust your budget as needed: Your budget is not set in stone and may need to be adjusted as your business grows and changes.

Creating a budget can help you stay organized, make informed financial decisions, and track your progress towards your financial goals. It can also help you identify areas where you can cut costs or increase revenue to improve your profitability.

PURCHASING A FOOD TRUCK

The food truck is the most critical component of your food truck business. Choosing the right vehicle to serve your customers' needs is essential for success. In this section, we will explore the key factors to consider when purchasing a food truck, including size, kitchen equipment, and mobility.

Types of food trucks

Food trucks come in many shapes and sizes, each designed to meet different needs and requirements. Here are some of the most common types of food trucks:

Standard food truck: A standard food truck is the most common type of food truck. It typically features a full kitchen and a serving window, making it easy to cook and serve food to customers.

Food trailer: A food trailer is similar to a food truck, but it is towed behind a vehicle. This type of food truck is often used for catering or events, as it can be easily transported to different locations.

Food cart: A food cart is a smaller, more mobile version of a food truck. It is typically used for selling food and beverages at events or in high-traffic areas.

Pop-up restaurant: A pop-up restaurant is a temporary food truck that operates in different locations for a limited time. This type of food truck is often used to test new menu items or to generate buzz for a new restaurant.

Specialized food truck: A specialized food truck focuses on a specific type of cuisine or food item, such as burgers, tacos, or ice cream. This type of food truck can be highly successful if it serves a popular and unique menu item.

When choosing a food truck, it's important to consider your menu, your target market, and your budget. Each type of food truck has its advantages and disadvantages, and it's important to choose the one that best fits your needs and goals.

Choosing the right food truck

Choosing the right food truck is important for the success of your food truck business. Here are some factors to consider when selecting a food truck:

Size: Choose a food truck that is large enough to accommodate your kitchen equipment and staff but small enough to be mobile and easily maneuvered on the road.

Kitchen equipment: Look for a food truck that has the necessary kitchen equipment to prepare your menu items, such as grills, fryers, refrigerators, and sinks. Make sure the equipment is in good working condition and meets health and safety standards.

Mobility: Choose a food truck that is mobile and easy to drive. Consider factors such as fuel efficiency, turning radius, and parking restrictions when selecting a food truck.

Customization: Look for a food truck that can be customized to meet your specific needs and branding requirements. Consider factors such as exterior design, graphics, and lighting to make your food truck stand out.

Budget: Choose a food truck that fits your budget. Consider both the initial purchase cost and ongoing maintenance and operating expenses when making your decision.

Warranty and support: Look for a food truck that comes with a warranty and reliable support from the manufacturer or dealer. This can provide peace of mind and ensure that any issues can be quickly addressed.

Choosing the right food truck can be a challenging process, but taking the time to research and evaluate your options can help ensure that you make the right choice for your business.

Equipment and supplies

Having the right equipment and supplies is crucial for the success of your food truck business. Here are some essential items you will need:

Cooking equipment: You will need cooking equipment such as grills, fryers, ovens, and burners to prepare your menu items. Choose equipment that is durable, easy to clean, and energy-efficient.

Refrigeration and storage: You will need refrigerators and freezers to keep your ingredients fresh and safe. You will also need storage space for dry goods and non-perishable items.

Utensils and cookware: You will need utensils such as knives, spatulas, tongs, and ladles, as well as cookware such as pots, pans, and baking sheets.

Serving and packaging supplies: You will need supplies such as plates, bowls, cups, and napkins for serving your food. You will also need packaging supplies such as food containers, bags, and wrappers for takeout orders.

Cleaning supplies: You will need cleaning supplies such as dish soap, sponges, towels, and sanitizers to keep your food truck clean and hygienic.

When selecting equipment and supplies, it's important to consider factors such as quality, durability, and ease of use. You may also need to consider space limitations and energy requirements when selecting equipment for your food truck.

It's a good idea to work with a reputable supplier who specializes in food truck equipment and supplies. They can help you choose the right items for your business and provide ongoing support and maintenance services.

BUILDING YOUR BRAND

Building a strong brand is essential for the success of any business, and this is particularly true for food truck businesses. In this section, we will explore the key elements of building a strong brand for your food truck, including creating a memorable brand identity, developing a unique menu, and marketing your business to attract and retain customers. By building a strong brand, you can differentiate your food truck from competitors and create a loyal following of customers who are passionate about your food and your brand.

Creating a brand identity

Creating a strong brand identity is a critical step in building a successful food truck business. Your brand identity is how customers perceive your business and what sets you apart from your competitors. Here are some key elements of creating a strong brand identity for your food truck:

Name and logo: Choose a memorable and unique name for your food truck that reflects your brand's personality and values. Your logo should be visually appealing and easily recognizable.

Color scheme and design: Choose a color scheme and design that is consistent with your brand's personality and values. Consider using design elements that evoke the type of cuisine you serve or the atmosphere you want to create.

Menu design: Your menu design should be clear, easy to read, and visually appealing. Consider using high-quality photos of your food to entice customers.

Social media presence: Your social media presence is an important part of your brand identity. Choose social media platforms that are relevant to your target audience and post engaging content that showcases your food and your brand.

Customer service: Your customer service is an essential part of your brand identity. Train your staff to provide friendly and efficient service that reflects your brand's values and personality.

By creating a strong brand identity, you can differentiate your food truck from competitors and create a memorable and engaging experience for your customers. Your brand identity should be consistent across all touchpoints, from your food truck's design to your social media presence and customer service.

Marketing your business

Marketing your food truck is critical to attract and retain customers. Here are some key elements of marketing your food truck:

Online presence: Your food truck should have a strong online presence to reach potential customers. This includes having a website, social media profiles, and online listings.

Social media marketing: Social media is a powerful tool for promoting your food truck. Share high-quality photos and videos of your food and events, engage with customers through comments and direct messages, and run targeted ads to reach new audiences.

Events and promotions: Participate in local events and promotions to get your food truck in front of new audiences. This can include food truck festivals, farmers markets, and catering events.

Referral marketing: Encourage satisfied customers to refer their friends and family to your food truck. Offer incentives such as discounts or free food for referrals.

Email marketing: Use email marketing to stay in touch with your customers and promote special events and promotions. Collect email addresses through your website and social media profiles.

By utilizing these marketing strategies, you can increase your food truck's visibility and attract new customers. It's important to track your marketing efforts to determine what is working and make adjustments as needed. With consistent and effective marketing, you can build a loyal following of customers who are passionate about your food and your brand.

Developing a social media strategy

Social media is a powerful tool for promoting your food truck and engaging with customers. To effectively leverage social media, it's important to develop a social media strategy that aligns with your overall business goals. Here are some key elements of developing a social media strategy for your food truck:

Choose the right platforms: There are many social media platforms available, each with its own strengths and weaknesses. Consider which platforms are most relevant to your target audience and focus your efforts on those platforms.

Define your target audience: Develop a clear understanding of your target audience, including their demographics, interests, and behaviors. This will help you create content that resonates with them and drives engagement.

Develop a content strategy: Create a content calendar that outlines the types of content you will share on each platform and when you will share it. This can include photos and videos of your food, behind-the-scenes content, and promotions and events.

Engage with your followers: Social media is a two-way conversation, so it's important to engage with your followers by responding to comments and direct messages, asking for feedback, and running polls and surveys.

Track your results: Use social media analytics to track your performance and adjust your strategy as needed. Pay attention to metrics such as engagement, reach, and conversion rates to understand what is working and what can be improved.

By developing a social media strategy, you can effectively leverage social media to promote your food truck, engage with customers, and drive business results. Be consistent in your approach, and don't be afraid to experiment with different types of content and tactics to find what works best for your business.

MENU DEVELOPMENT AND PRICING

Crafting a menu that showcases your culinary expertise and meets the needs of your target audience is a critical component of launching a successful food truck business. Menu development and pricing can make or break your food truck, as it can influence customer satisfaction, profitability, and brand reputation. In this section, we will explore some key considerations for menu development and pricing in the food truck industry. From developing a concept to pricing your menu items, we will cover everything you need to know to create a menu that will drive sales and delight your customers.

Designing your menu

Designing a menu for your food truck is an important part of creating a successful business. Your menu should reflect your culinary vision and showcase your unique offerings. Here are some key considerations to keep in mind when designing your menu:

Develop a concept: Your menu should align with your overall food truck concept. Consider the types of food you want to serve, the cooking techniques you will use, and the overall vibe of your truck. Use this information to develop a menu that reflects your brand and appeals to your target audience.

Keep it simple: Your menu should be easy to read and understand. Avoid overloading your menu with too many options or complicated descriptions. Stick to simple, easy-to-understand language, and use high-quality images to showcase your dishes.

Offer a variety of options: While simplicity is important, you should also aim to offer a variety of options to appeal to different tastes and dietary needs. Consider offering vegetarian or gluten-free options, and make sure you have a good mix of entrees, sides, and desserts.

Use local ingredients: Using locally-sourced ingredients can be a great way to differentiate your menu and showcase your commitment to sustainability. Consider partnering with local farmers or vendors to source fresh, high-quality ingredients.

Consider seasonality: Seasonal ingredients can add variety and freshness to your menu. Consider updating your menu seasonally to showcase the best ingredients available.

Designing a menu can be a fun and creative process, but it's important to keep your target audience in mind and stay true to your brand. By offering a variety of options, using local ingredients, and keeping your menu simple and easy to read, you can create a menu that will drive sales and delight your customers.

Sourcing ingredients

Sourcing high-quality ingredients is crucial to the success of any food business, and it's particularly important for food trucks. With limited space and resources, food truck operators need to be strategic about ingredient sourcing to ensure they have everything they need to create delicious, high-quality dishes. Here are some tips for sourcing ingredients for your food truck:

Develop relationships with local suppliers: Building relationships with local farmers, distributors, and other suppliers can help you secure high-quality ingredients at a reasonable cost. Consider attending local farmers markets or networking events to meet potential suppliers and build relationships.

Use seasonal ingredients: Seasonal ingredients are often fresher, more flavorful, and less expensive than out-of-season produce. By focusing on seasonal ingredients, you can create a more sustainable menu and showcase the best ingredients available.

Consider food safety: When sourcing ingredients, it's important to consider food safety. Make sure you are purchasing ingredients from reputable suppliers and that all ingredients are properly stored and handled to prevent contamination.

Purchase in bulk: Purchasing ingredients in bulk can help you save money and ensure you have enough ingredients on hand to meet demand. Consider partnering with other food truck operators or restaurants to purchase ingredients in bulk and split the cost.

Consider specialty ingredients: Depending on your menu, you may need to source specialty ingredients that are not widely available. Consider partnering with specialty distributors or ordering ingredients online to ensure you have everything you need to create your dishes.

By being strategic about ingredient sourcing, you can create a menu that showcases high-quality, fresh ingredients and sets your food truck apart from the competition. Consider building relationships with local suppliers, using seasonal ingredients, and purchasing in bulk to keep your costs low and your menu fresh and delicious.

Pricing your menu items

Pricing your menu items is a critical aspect of running a successful food truck business. You want to ensure that you are covering your costs and making a profit, while also keeping your prices competitive and attractive to customers. Here are some tips for pricing your menu items:

Know your costs: Before you can set your prices, you need to know your costs. Calculate the cost of all your ingredients, as well as overhead costs like equipment, labor, and permits. This will help you determine your break-even point and set your prices accordingly.

Consider your competition: Look at other food trucks and restaurants in your area to get an idea of what they are charging for similar menu items. Consider how your prices compare and whether you need to adjust your prices to stay competitive.

Price for profit: It's important to set your prices so that you are making a profit. This means charging more than your costs, but not so much that customers are deterred from purchasing your menu items. Consider adding a markup of 30-40% to cover your costs and make a profit.

Use psychological pricing: Psychological pricing strategies, such as pricing items at $9.99 instead of $10.00, can make your menu items more attractive to customers. Consider using these strategies to make your prices more appealing.

Offer specials: Offering specials or promotions can help attract customers and increase sales. Consider offering daily or weekly specials, or discounts for bulk orders or frequent customers.

By knowing your costs, considering your competition, pricing for profit, using psychological pricing, and offering specials, you can set prices that are attractive to customers while also ensuring that your food truck business is profitable. It's important to regularly review and adjust your prices as needed to stay competitive and profitable.

OPERATIONS AND MANAGEMENT

Once you have your food truck business up and running, it's important to focus on operations and management to ensure that you are providing high-quality food and service to your customers. This includes everything from managing your inventory to training your staff to providing excellent customer service. In this section, we will cover some of the key aspects of operations and management that are essential for running a successful food truck business.

Managing inventory

Managing inventory is an essential part of running a successful food truck business. You want to ensure that you have enough ingredients and supplies on hand to meet customer demand, while also minimizing waste and keeping costs under control. Here are some tips for effective inventory management:

Track your inventory: Keep track of your inventory by using inventory software or spreadsheets. This will help you monitor your stock levels and identify when you need to order more supplies.

Use the FIFO method: FIFO stands for "first in, first out." This means that you should use the oldest ingredients first to prevent waste and spoilage.

Order in bulk: Ordering ingredients and supplies in bulk can help you save money and reduce your overall costs.

Minimize waste: Monitor your inventory regularly to identify any ingredients or supplies that are going unused or nearing their expiration dates. This will help you minimize waste and reduce your costs.

Use a par level system: A par level system involves setting a minimum inventory level for each ingredient or supply, so that you know when it's time to reorder. This helps ensure that you always have enough inventory on hand to meet customer demand.

By effectively managing your inventory, you can reduce waste, control costs, and ensure that you have enough supplies on hand to provide high-quality food and service to your customers.

Hiring and training staff

Hiring and training staff is an important aspect of running a successful food truck business. Here are some tips to help you find and train the right employees:

Create job descriptions: Clearly define the roles and responsibilities of each position, including requirements for experience and skills.

Recruit the right candidates: Post job openings on job boards, social media, and industry-specific websites. Be sure to review resumes and conduct thorough interviews to find the best candidates.

Train your staff: Provide comprehensive training to new employees, including information about food safety and handling, customer service, and the specifics of your menu and operations.

Foster a positive work environment: Encourage teamwork and positive communication among your staff. This can help create a positive work environment and improve customer satisfaction.

Provide ongoing training and support: Schedule regular training sessions and provide ongoing support to your staff. This can help them improve their skills and stay motivated on the job.

Offer incentives and rewards: Consider offering incentives and rewards to your staff for meeting performance goals or providing exceptional service. This can help motivate your employees and improve overall job satisfaction.

By hiring and training the right staff, you can improve customer service, increase sales, and ensure that your food truck business runs smoothly and efficiently.

Managing day-to-day operations

Managing day-to-day operations is critical to the success of your food truck business. Here are some tips for ensuring your operations run smoothly:

Create a schedule: Develop a schedule for opening and closing, food prep, and restocking inventory. Stick to the schedule as much as possible to ensure consistency in operations.

Maintain equipment: Regularly clean and maintain all equipment to prevent breakdowns and ensure food safety. Schedule routine maintenance and repairs to keep equipment in good working condition.

Monitor inventory: Keep track of inventory levels and reorder supplies as needed. This will help prevent running out of key ingredients and supplies.

Stay organized: Develop a system for organizing food and supplies to ensure easy access and efficient operations. Use containers and labels to keep everything organized.

Manage cash flow: Keep track of all expenses and revenue to ensure your business stays profitable. Use a budget to manage expenses and avoid overspending.

Provide excellent customer service: Make sure your staff is friendly and helpful to customers. Respond promptly to customer feedback and complaints to ensure customer satisfaction.

By implementing these strategies, you can ensure that your food truck business runs efficiently and provides excellent service to your customers. This can help you build a loyal customer base and increase your profits over time.

FINANCIAL MANAGEMENT

Financial management is a crucial aspect of running any business, including a food truck business. It involves planning, organizing, and controlling the financial resources of your business to ensure profitability and growth. Effective financial management can help you make informed decisions and maximize profits. In this section, we will explore some key financial management strategies that can help you run a successful food truck business.

Tracking revenue and expenses

Tracking revenue and expenses is a crucial part of financial management for any food truck business. By keeping accurate records of your income and expenses, you can gain valuable insights into the financial health of your business and make informed decisions about how to manage your finances. Here are some tips for tracking revenue and expenses:

Use accounting software: Accounting software like QuickBooks or FreshBooks can help you keep track of your income and expenses, generate financial reports, and manage your budget.

Separate personal and business finances: It's essential to keep your personal and business finances separate. Use a separate bank account and credit card for your business expenses to make tracking easier.

Keep receipts: Keep receipts for all expenses, including food and supplies, equipment, and vehicle maintenance. This will help you accurately track expenses and claim tax deductions.

Track daily sales: Keep track of daily sales to monitor revenue and identify trends in customer behavior. Use a point-of-sale system to streamline the process and get real-time data.

Review financial statements regularly: Review your financial statements regularly to monitor revenue, expenses, and profits. This will help you identify areas where you can cut costs or increase revenue.

By tracking your revenue and expenses consistently, you can gain a clear understanding of your financial situation and make informed decisions about how to manage your business finances. This can help you maintain profitability and grow your business over time.

Managing cash flow

Managing cash flow is a crucial part of financial management for any food truck business. Cash flow refers to the movement of money in and out of your business over a specific period. Proper cash flow management can help you ensure that you have enough cash on hand to pay your bills, buy supplies, and cover other expenses. Here are some tips for managing cash flow in your food truck business:

Create a cash flow statement: A cash flow statement shows the movement of cash in and out of your business over a specific period. It helps you identify periods where you may have more cash going out than coming in, and vice versa.

Forecast your cash flow: Use your historical cash flow data to create a forecast of your future cash flow. This will help you identify periods where you may have cash shortages and plan accordingly.

Manage your expenses: Managing your expenses is crucial for maintaining positive cash flow. Keep track of your expenses, and try to find ways to cut costs wherever possible.

Invoice promptly: If you have a customer or client who owes you money, invoice them promptly. This will help you avoid cash flow problems and ensure that you have enough cash on hand to pay your bills.

Negotiate payment terms: Negotiate favorable payment terms with your suppliers and vendors. This can help you manage your cash flow by giving you more time to pay your bills.

By managing your cash flow effectively, you can ensure that you have enough cash on hand to cover your expenses and grow your business over time.

Tax considerations

As a food truck business owner, it's essential to understand the various tax considerations that come with running your business. Here are some important tax considerations to keep in mind:

Sales tax: Depending on the state and city where your food truck operates, you may be required to collect and remit sales tax on the items you sell. Make sure you understand the sales tax rules in your area and keep detailed records of your sales and tax collected.

Income tax: As a business owner, you will need to file an annual income tax return with the IRS. You may also be required to make quarterly estimated tax payments throughout the year. Consider working with an accountant to help you file your taxes accurately and minimize your tax liability.

Payroll taxes: If you have employees, you will need to withhold payroll taxes from their paychecks and remit those taxes to the appropriate government agencies. You may also be required to pay unemployment and workers' compensation taxes.

Property taxes: If you own the land or building where you operate your food truck business, you will need to pay property taxes on that property.

Deductions: As a business owner, you may be able to take deductions for certain business expenses, such as equipment purchases, supplies, and vehicle expenses. Keep detailed records of your expenses and work with an accountant to ensure you are taking advantage of all available deductions.

Make sure you understand your tax obligations as a food truck business owner and keep accurate records of your income and expenses. By staying on top of your tax obligations, you can avoid penalties and fees and ensure that your business stays in good standing with the government.

GROWING YOUR FOOD TRUCK BUSINESS

Congratulations on successfully starting and managing your food truck business! Now, it's time to explore opportunities for growth and expansion. In this section, we will discuss various strategies and techniques that can help you take your business to the next level. Whether you want to expand your food truck fleet, open a brick-and-mortar restaurant, or introduce new menu items, this section will provide you with valuable insights and tips to help you achieve your goals.

Expanding your menu

One way to grow your food truck business is to expand your menu. You can introduce new dishes, seasonal items, or limited-time offers to keep your customers engaged and interested. When adding new items to your menu, it's important to consider your target market's preferences and dietary restrictions.

To start, you can conduct a survey or gather feedback from your regular customers to understand their favorite dishes and what they would like to see on your menu. Additionally, you can research industry trends and keep an eye on what your competitors are offering to identify any gaps in the market.

Once you have identified potential menu items, you should test them out to see how they perform. You can offer samples or limited-time offers to gauge customer interest and obtain feedback. It's also essential to consider the cost of ingredients and labor when adding new menu items to ensure that they are profitable.

When introducing new menu items, it's essential to market them effectively. You can promote them on your social media platforms, use eye-catching graphics or images, and offer discounts or special deals to encourage customers to try them out. Finally, always monitor your sales and customer feedback to adjust your menu accordingly and maintain customer satisfaction.

Catering and events

Another way to grow your food truck business is to offer catering services and participate in events. Catering can be a lucrative source of revenue for your food truck, especially for corporate events, weddings, and private parties.

To get started with catering, you can create a separate catering menu that offers a variety of dishes suitable for larger groups. You can also create packages that include different food options, such as appetizers, entrees, and desserts. Be sure to price your catering menu items accordingly, taking into account the cost of ingredients, labor, and any additional equipment or rentals required for the event.

To market your catering services, you can leverage your existing customer base and social media platforms to spread the word. You can also attend local networking events or reach out to event planners to establish relationships and generate new leads.

In addition to catering, participating in events such as food festivals, farmers' markets, and community events can also help grow your business. These events can expose your brand to new customers and provide an opportunity to test out new menu items and receive feedback.

When participating in events, it's essential to plan ahead and be

prepared. Make sure to have enough food and supplies on hand, arrive early to set up your truck and display, and have a system in place for handling transactions and managing lines. Additionally, it's crucial to provide excellent customer service and maintain a positive and engaging presence at the event to leave a lasting impression on potential customers.

Opening a brick-and-mortar location

If your food truck business has been successful, you may consider expanding by opening a brick-and-mortar location. This can provide you with a more stable and consistent revenue stream, and allow you to reach a larger customer base. Here are some things to consider when opening a physical location:

Location: Finding the right location is crucial for any brick-and-mortar business. Look for a place that is easily accessible and has plenty of foot traffic. Consider the demographics of the area and whether it aligns with your target market.

Lease or buy: Determine whether you want to lease or buy the property. Leasing can be a good option if you want to test the waters before committing to a long-term investment. Buying may be a better option if you are confident in your business and have the capital to invest.

Design and layout: The design and layout of your restaurant should reflect your brand and the type of food you serve. Consider hiring a professional interior designer to help you create a space that is both functional and visually appealing.

Equipment and supplies: You will need to purchase kitchen equipment and supplies, such as refrigerators, ovens, and utensils. Research suppliers and compare prices to find the best deals.

Staffing: You will need to hire additional staff to manage the restaurant. Consider creating job descriptions, conducting interviews, and providing training to ensure that your staff is knowledgeable and efficient.

Permits and licenses: You will need to obtain permits and licenses for your restaurant, such as a food service permit, liquor license, and business license. Research the requirements in your area and ensure that you comply with all regulations.

Marketing: You may already have a strong brand and customer base from your food truck business, but you will still need to market your new location to attract customers. Develop a marketing strategy that includes online and offline advertising, social media, and promotions.

Opening a brick-and-mortar location can be a significant investment, but it can also provide a platform for long-term growth and success.

CONCLUSION

Starting a food truck business can be an exciting and rewarding venture, but it requires careful planning, hard work, and a commitment to excellence. By following the steps outlined in this guide, you can lay the groundwork for a successful food truck business that meets the needs of your target market, provides a high-quality product, and builds a strong brand reputation. Remember, the food truck industry is constantly evolving, so be open to new ideas, adapt to changes in the market, and stay focused on your goals. With the right approach and a passion for food and entrepreneurship, you can build a thriving food truck business that brings joy and satisfaction to both you and your customers.

Challenges and rewards of running a food truck business

Running a food truck business can be both challenging and rewarding. On one hand, food truck owners face numerous obstacles that can make it difficult to achieve success. These challenges can include:

Seasonal changes: Depending on the location, food truck businesses can experience fluctuations in business due to seasonal changes. For example, in areas with harsh winters, business may slow down during the colder months.

Finding a good location: Securing a prime location can be challenging, as some areas may be already saturated with food trucks, or the competition may be tough.

Permits and regulations: Obtaining the necessary permits and complying with health and safety regulations can be a time-consuming and complicated process.

Weather conditions: Outdoor events can be affected by weather conditions such as rain, heat, or wind, which can reduce foot traffic and affect sales.

Despite these challenges, there are also many rewards to running a food truck business. Some of these rewards include:

Flexibility: Food truck businesses offer more flexibility than traditional brick-and-mortar restaurants. Owners can change their location and hours of operation more easily to adapt to changing conditions.

Lower overhead costs: Compared to a traditional restaurant, a food truck has lower overhead costs, including rent, utilities, and maintenance expenses.

Creative expression: Food trucks allow owners to express their creativity through unique menu offerings and eye-catching designs.

Strong customer relationships: Food truck businesses offer the opportunity to build strong relationships with customers by providing personalized service and a unique experience.

Running a food truck business can be a challenging but rewarding experience for entrepreneurs who are willing to put in the hard work and dedication necessary to succeed.

www.ingramcontent.com/pod-product-compliance
Lightning Source LLC
Chambersburg PA
CBHW070859220526
45466CB00005B/2054